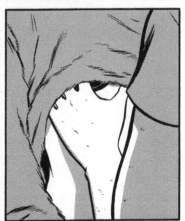

...AS THE U.N. DEADLINE FOR AN IRAQI WITHDRAWAL APPROACHES, PRESIDENT BUSH HAS NOW ORDERED OVER 400,000 U.S. TROOPS INTO THE PERSIAN GULF...

LOOK AT THIS... THEY COULD RE-INSTATE THE DRAFT ANY DAY NOW AND WE'D BE *FUCKED!*

AREN'T WE TOO YOUNG?

THERE WERE GUYS WHO WERE ONLY SEVENTEEN AT THE START OF VIETNAM...NEXT THING THEY KNOW, THEY'RE GETTING *EVISCERATED* IN SAIGON!

I'M *SIXTEEN.*

WELL, IF THIS GOES ON LONG ENOUGH...

JEEZ...I GUESS I'D HAVE TO HIDE OUT IN CANADA OR SOMETHING...

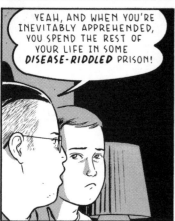

YEAH, AND WHEN YOU'RE INEVITABLY APPREHENDED, YOU SPEND THE REST OF YOUR LIFE IN SOME *DISEASE-RIDDLED* PRISON!

I'D BLOW MY OWN BRAINS OUT BEFORE I FOUGHT IN SOME WAR.

PSHHT

HERE... JUST TRY ONE SIP.

NO.

OKAY...THIS IS THE DRUM MACHINE. YOU JUST HIT THESE PADS...

AND YOU CAN LOOP IT.

BOOM BOOM TCH!

BA-BOOM TCH! BA-BOOM BOOM TCH

HERE'S THE SAMPLER. SAY SOMETHING INTO THE MIC.

LIKE WHAT?

ANYTHING! JUST SAY, UH..."MY NAME IS SCOTTY, AND I'LL DO ANYTHING WITH ANYONE."

OR WHATEVER. IT'S INCONSEQUENTIAL.

MY NAME IS SCOTTY, AND I'LL DO ANYTHING WITH ANYONE...?

HA HA

OKAY, LET'S GET THE DRUMS GOING AGAIN... PLAY SOME CHORDS...

BA-BOOM  BA-BOOM
BOOM  BA
TCH!  TCH!

AND NOW WHEN-EVER WE HIT THIS BUTTON...

BA-BOOM
BOOM TCH!

MY NAME IS SCOTTY, AND I'LL DO ANYTHING WITH ANYONE...?

HA HA
HA HA HA

BA-BOOM  BA-BOOM
TCH!  BOOM  TC

WE SHOULD GET BACK. PEOPLE ARE PROBABLY WONDERING WHAT HAPPENED TO US.

I DOUBT IT.

I WANNA GO FOR A SWIM...

WHOAH

CAREFUL...

LOOK AT THAT FUCKING SMILE.

WELL?

LOOK, I'M NOT GONNA GO INTO DETAIL OR ANYTHING, BUT UH... SHE SWALLOWS.

FUCK YOU!

SHIT... CHECK HER OUT NOW.

3

HOW ABOUT YOU? WHAT DID YOU DO TONIGHT?

OH, I MET A FRIEND FROM WORK FOR COFFEE.

IT WAS NICE.

WELL, I'M GONNA PUT MY HEADPHONES ON AND GO TO BED...

SLEEP TIGHT.

BOYS' LOCKER ROOM

I FEEL LIKE I CAN LITERALLY **SMELL** THE BACTERIA WAFTING AROUND ME...

THANK **GOD** THIS IS THE LAST SEMESTER OF THIS TORTURE I'LL EVER HAVE TO ENDURE!

WHAT AM **I** GONNA DO NEXT YEAR? MAYBE I CAN GET SOME KIND OF DOCTOR'S EXCUSE...

"OH, ALEXTH...I'M GETTING **THO** HORNY!"

HA HA HA

"ME TOO, THCOTTY!"

"I'D TAKE A THOWER, BUT I'M AFRAID EVERYONE WILL THEE MY HARD-ON!"

HA HA HA HA

HEY GUYS... ENJOYING THE SHOW?

CAREFUL, BRYAN... THEY MIGHT DOUBLE-TEAM YOU!

I'M JUST **DYING** FOR ONE OF THESE STEROID-INJECTED **FUCKS** TO THREATEN ME PHYSICALLY...

WHAT ARE YOU TALKING ABOUT?

BECAUSE THEN I WOULD BE LEGALLY ENTITLED TO USE **THIS**...

5

YOU'RE CARRYING AROUND A *GUN*?

WOULD YOU SHUT UP?

IT'S A *TASER*. TEN SECONDS OF CONTACT AND YOUR ADVERSARY IS INCAPACITATED. TWENTY SECONDS AND THEY'RE UNCONSCIOUS.

*KOFF KOFF*aggots

HA HA HA HA

HI CAMMIE!

OH...HEY, SCOTTY. GOD, HOW LATE AM I?

ONLY LIKE TWENTY MINUTES. IT'S BEEN PRETTY DEAD ANYWAY...

MY HEAD *KILLS*... I PARTIED WAY TOO MUCH LAST NIGHT.

YEAH...

CAN I ASK YOU SOMETHING? YOU'RE FRIENDS WITH BRYAN VANDERMEER, RIGHT?

WE HANG OUT.

HOW CAN YOU *STAND* THAT GUY? I MEAN...

BRYAN? HE'S OKAY.

WELL, THE NEXT TIME HE MAKES SOME FAG JOKE ABOUT ME, REMIND HIM THAT *HE'S* THE ONE ROLLING AROUND WITH GUYS ON THE WRESTLING TEAM.

YOU KNOW, IT'S NOT REALLY *YOU* HE'S MAKING FUN OF, IT'S MORE LIKE YOU AND THAT ALEX GUY...TOGETHER.

OH...WELL THAT CHANGES EVERYTHING!

PFF...

SO, THEN...YOU AND ALEX...

AREN'T...?

OH MY GOD!

DO PEOPLE SERIOUSLY THINK WE'RE *GAY*? WHAT... JUST BECAUSE WE'RE NOT OBNOXIOUS, ATHLETIC JERKS LIKE BRYAN?

IT'S JUST THAT YOU TWO ARE *ALWAYS* TOGETHER, AND YOU NEVER HANG AROUND WITH ANY GIRLS...YOU JUST SEEM LIKE A...COUPLE!

LOOK, JUST BECAUSE WE'RE EACH OTHER'S ONLY FRIEND, THAT *DOES NOT MAKE US*—

SHHH

IT DOES NOT MAKE US HOMOS.

OKAY, OKAY.

MOM?

ARE YOU GONNA EAT ANY OF THIS PASTA?

WHAT?

NO...YOU GO AHEAD.

IS THAT GUY PICKING YOU UP?

HIS NAME'S *PHIL*, AND NO...I'M MEETING HIM AT THE THEATER.

I THINK ALEX SAID SOMETHING ABOUT GOING TO SOME... PARTY.

SO IF IT ENDS UP GETTING LATE, I MIGHT JUST CRASH AT HIS PLACE.

THAT'S FINE.

MM... SMELLS GOOD.

I'M GLAD THAT YOU'RE GOING TO PARTIES AND HAVING FUN.

WELL... WE'LL SEE ABOUT THE "FUN" PART.

SO, ARE THERE GONNA BE PEOPLE FROM SCHOOL THERE?

YOU **MUST** BE JOKING.

SUTTER HIGH IS AN **INFINITESIMAL** PART OF MY WORLD.

BANG! BANG! K-CLANG CLANG BANG!

K-CLANG CLANG ANG!

DOES ANYBODY HAVE ANY... ANY BREAD? MY TOFU DOGS ARE GETTING ALL BURNT!

HOW ABOUT A... A PLATE OR SOME-THING?

I CAN'T BELIEVE YOU'VE NEVER HEARD THIS!

IT'S, LIKE, THE HEAVIEST JAPANESE NOISE STUFF EVER RECORDED!

OOH... IS THAT ROBITUSSIN?

BANG K-CLAN CLA

HEY, SCOTTY. HAVE A SEAT.

DID YOU MANAGE TO FIND THE LAVATORY?

YEAH... DOWNSTAIRS.

WE'RE JUST WATCHING THE MAYHEM ON CNN...

WHAT YOU'RE SEEING IS LIVE FOOTAGE OF THE SCUD MISSILE IN ACTION.

THIS IS BEING FILMED WITH NIGHT VISION CAMERAS...ACTUAL VISIBILITY IS CONSIDERABLY— OH! ANOTHER BIG HIT!

IT JUST LOOKS LIKE A VIDEO GAME.

HEY, SCOTTY... COME FEEL THIS. MELANIE JUST SHAVED HER HEAD.

YOU DON'T MIND... RIGHT, MEL?

I...

I WANT TO WATCH THIS.

HAHA

OKAY, OKAY...

HEY BRYAN!

WHOO!

CLAP!
CLAP!
CLAP!

CLAP!

YEAH!

CLAP! CLAP! CLAP!

GOD, I'M SICK OF THAT FUCKING SLUT-FACE!

LIKE THEY HAVEN'T SEEN *THAT* BEFORE...

ALL RIGHT... A DEAL'S A DEAL.

I DON'T NEED A CUP!

GLUG

ARE YOU ALREADY ASLEEP?

WHAT...?

YOU'RE LUCKY YOU CAN FALL ASLEEP SO QUICKLY.

HOW'S THE BED?

OKAY...

IT'S WEIRD TO THINK MY PARENTS USED TO FUCK RIGHT HERE.

EHK, JESUS... WHAT TIME IS IT?

ONLY ABOUT TWO... TWO-THIRTY...

I APOLOGIZE FOR WAKING YOU UP. GO BACK TO SLEEP.

≈SNIFF≈

≈SNIFF≈

≈SNIFF≈

UH, BRYAN...? CAN YOU COME HERE FOR A SEC?

WHAT'S UP?

WELL, CAMMIE'S PASSED OUT AND SHE, UH... SHE SMELLS LIKE SHIT.

WHAT?

SQUEEK! SQUEEK!

PSSSHHHHHH

THEY'RE IN HERE!

CHECK HER OUT!

HA HA HA

WHAT'S GOING ON?

LET ME SEE!

IS SHE OKAY?

SHE'S NOT WAKING UP.

WE BETTER CALL 911.

I'LL, UH... SEE YOU AT SCHOOL.

OF COURSE.

SLAM!

IT'S ME.

HELLO?

15

MOM?

OH MY GOD, CAMMIE... HOW *ARE* YOU?

I'M FINE. IT WAS NOTHING A LITTLE STOMACH-PUMPING COULDN'T FIX.

HA HA

HEY, BRYAN. I GUESS I'M THE TALK OF THE SCHOOL THANKS TO YOU.

UM...I THINK HE'S WAITING FOR AN APOLOGY.

HA HA

*YOU* EXPECT AN APOLOGY FROM *ME*?

I THINK THAT'S KINDA WHAT YOU DO WHEN YOU SMEAR DIARRHEA ON SOMEONE'S COUCH.

HA HA

SNORT

FUCK OFF, BRYAN. HOW ABOUT *YOU* APOLOGIZING FOR TAKING MY CLOTHES OFF AND INVITING EVERYONE IN FOR A LOOK?

YOU DON'T EVEN KNOW WHAT HAPPENED, BITCH. I PROBABLY SAVED YOUR FUCKING LIFE.

AND WHERE WERE *YOU* AT LUNCH TODAY?

I COULDN'T FIND YOU.

YEAH...I HAD TO FINISH THIS ASSIGNMENT FOR PHOTO. SO I WAS IN THE DARKROOM.

SOU

HI! HOW'S IT GOING? I -

I DON'T WANT TO TALK ABOUT IT.

OKAY.

Sorry...We're CLOSED

17

NO, NO...IT WOULDN'T BE LIKE HITTING "PAUSE" ON THE VCR. I MEAN, EVERYTHING WOULD STILL BE MOVING AROUND...

IT'S JUST LIKE... EVERYTHING STAYS BASICALLY THE SAME. NO AGING, NO DYING, NO BIG CHANGES...

GOD...THAT'S A PRETTY FUCKED-UP FANTASY.

WELL, I JUST THINK ABOUT IT SOMETIMES.

AND YOU'D WANT THIS TO HAPPEN, LIKE, NOW?

NO WAY!

MORE LIKE... FOUR OR FIVE YEARS AGO.

THAT SEEMS LIKE A GOOD TIME TO FREEZE.

WHAT ABOUT NEW EXPERIENCES?

YEAH...

I GUESS I'M JUST NOT INTO THAT.

WHAT?

I KNOW, I KNOW...

I'M PROBABLY THE ONLY 16-YEAR-OLD IN THE WORLD THAT DOESN'T WANT TO GET DRUNK AND DO DRUGS AND GET LAID.

WAIT...

YOU DON'T WANT TO GET *LAID*?

I MEAN, IN THEORY... MAYBE. IT JUST SEEMS TOO MONUMENTAL.

HA HA HA

GOD...I'M HORNY ALL THE TIME! DON'T YOU EVER AT LEAST, UH...

WHAT?

YOU KNOW...

TCH... *NO!*

OH, YOU'RE SO FULL OF SHIT! I'VE GOT A LITTLE BROTHER...I KNOW HOW IT IS!

I'M SERIOUS.

I THINK I JUST ANALYZE EVERY-THING TOO MUCH.

I KNOW! YOU'RE LIKE SOME WEIRD ROBOT OR SOMETHING.

WHAT ARE YOU DOING AT LUNCH TOMORROW?

I DON'T KNOW. NOTHING.

COME TO THE ART ROOM. YOU CAN HELP ME WITH SOMETHING.

VOTE

VOTE

CAMMIE

VOTE

4 TREA$URER

ARE YOU KIDDING?

WHAT? THIS IS, LIKE, *CRUCIAL* TO ME GETTING INTO A GOOD COLLEGE.

THE WHOLE SCHOOL ELECTION THING JUST SEEMS KIND OF RETARDED.

IT'S *TOTALLY* RETARDED, BUT I CAN'T JUST COAST ON MY GRADES LIKE YOU.

BESIDES...WORKING ON THESE POSTERS IS ALSO A PERFECT EXCUSE FOR AVOIDING CERTAIN PEOPLE FOR AWHILE.

WELL, I'M INTO *THAT*.

OH YEAH?

LET'S JUST SAY THAT YOU AND YOUR FRIENDS WERE PROBABLY RIGHT ABOUT ALEX AFTER ALL.

19

ARE YOU SERIOUS? DID HE "COME OUT" TO YOU?

NOT EXACTLY... BUT HE ASKED ME TO SPEND THE NIGHT AT HIS PLACE LAST WEEKEND.

I GUESS THAT'S KIND OF GAY.

AND THEN HE KEPT SHOWING ME THESE, UH...PORNOS.

GAY PORN?

UH, NO... BUT THERE WERE GUYS IN IT.

HMM...

BUT LISTEN... I WOKE UP IN THE MIDDLE OF THE NIGHT, AND HE WAS, UH...

OH MY GOD. WHAT?

HE WAS...TRYING TO UNZIP MY PANTS. I STOPPED HIM, OBVIOUSLY, BUT...

NO WAY!

R-RING!

R-RING!

IT'S ALEX AGAIN.

I'M NOT HERE.

I'M SORRY... HE MUST'VE GONE TO WORK.

OKAY, I'LL TELL HIM.

BYE-BYE.

SO, WHAT'S GOING ON?

NOTHING.

JUST SORT OF A FALLING OUT, I GUESS.

WELL, IF BY SOME MIRACLE YOU FEEL LIKE TALKING ABOUT IT...

I KNOW. IT'S FINE.

I'VE GOT TO JUMP IN THE SHOWER, BUT IF PHIL SHOWS UP, LET HIM IN.

AND BE NICE!

UH, HI...

HI! YOU MUST BE SCOTTY, RIGHT? I'M PHIL.

YEAH... COME ON IN. MY MOM'S STILL GETTING READY.

GREAT.

YOUR MOM TOLD ME THAT YOU'RE REALLY INTO MUSIC.

YEAH.

WELL, HERE... THIS IS FOR YOU.

OH...

C+C music factory

GONNA MAKE YOU SWEAT

THANKS, BUT... I'M NOT REALLY INTO THESE GUYS.

WELL, THEY TOLD ME IT'S NUMBER ONE RIGHT NOW.

I KNOW IT'S POPULAR, BUT...

LOOK... JUST TAKE THE GOD DAMN TAPE, OKAY?

21

Scotty—
It's a terrible feeling when you have to try to avoid someone constantly, so don't worry about it. I'll make it easy and avoid you. Who would've thought that you'd try to climb the social ladder? Well, good luck... I know how bothersome those "fag" jokes can be. By the way, I'm not exactly sure what you've been telling people, but we both know what happened that night. Eventually you'll look back on all this with embarrassment and guilt, but for now, enjoy yourself.
Alex

YOU DIDN'T HEAR ABOUT THIS? HE GOT EXPELLED!

ARE YOU SERIOUS? WHEN?

YESTERDAY. I GUESS HE, LIKE, THREATENED BRYAN WITH A GUN.

OH, MAN...

HE SHOWED ME THAT THING BEFORE...IT'S NOT EVEN A REAL GUN! IT'S A...LEGAL SELF-DEFENSE THING.

WELL, I HEARD THAT THEY SEARCHED HIS LOCKER AND FOUND A GUN.

EITHER WAY... WHAT A PSYCHO.

I'M HOME!

SCOTTY, CAN YOU HELP ME WITH THE—

OH, I'M SORRY!

MOM, THIS IS CAMMIE. WE'RE WORKING ON A SPEECH...FOR SCHOOL...

HI!

CAMMIE...? IT'S VERY NICE TO MEET YOU.

THE NEXT CANDIDATE FOR TREASURER IS... CAMMIE SHAW.

CLAP! CLAP! CLAP! CLAP! CLAP! CLAP! CLAP! CL

CLAP! CLAP! CLAP! CLAP!

THANK YOU! FOR THOSE OF YOU WHO DON'T KNOW ME, LET ME—

THUD!

UM...

HAHA HAHAHA HA HA

HAHA HAHA HAHA HAHAHA HA

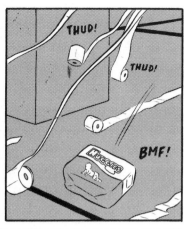

THUD!

THUD!

BMF!

HAHA HAHA HAHA HAHA CLAP! CLAP! HAHAHA HAHA HAHA CLAP! CLAP! HA

HAHA HAHA CLAP! CLAP! CLAP! HAHA HAHA CLAP! CLAP! HAHA

EXIT

CAMMIE! WAIT UP!

I DON'T EVEN KNOW WHY I'M SURPRISED...

I GUESS I'D PROBABLY THINK IT WAS PRETTY FUNNY IF IT WASN'T ME.

MAYBE YOU NEED TO RE-THINK SOME THINGS. I MEAN, THIS WOULDN'T HAVE HAPPENED IF YOU DIDN'T GET SO DRUNK AT THAT PARTY, RIGHT?

GOD, I KNOW. AND I DON'T EVEN *LIKE* JAGERMEISTER!

HA HA

IT'S NOT FUNNY! WHAT DO YOU EXPECT WHEN YOU GET DRUNK ALL THE TIME AND HANG OUT WITH THOSE KIND OF—

JESUS CHRIST!

WHY DON'T YOU GIVE ME A BREAK AND SHUT THE FUCK UP, OKAY SCOTTY?

25

THIS IS JUST ANOTHER CRAPPY THING IN MY LIFE THAT I'LL EVENTUALLY...

WHAT ARE YOU DOING?

I DON'T KNOW...

≶SNIFF≷ I'M JUST...

GOD, WHAT'S **WRONG** WITH YOU? **I'M** THE ONE THAT JUST GOT TOTALLY HUMILIATED!

I'M JUST... SORRY THIS HAPPENED...

DO YOU HAVE A CLASS WITH HER?

YEAH, BUT MAINLY I KNOW HER FROM THE RESTAURANT.

WELL, SHE SEEMS VERY SWEET.

I GUESS.

MAYBE YOU'D WANT TO INVITE HER OVER FOR DINNER SOME-TIME. WE CAN MAKE TACOS OR...

MOM.

I WAS JUST HELPING HER WITH A SPEECH, OKAY?

THAT'S FINE.

...WE HAVE REPORTS TONIGHT THAT SADDAM HUSSEIN HAS ORDERED A FULL WITHDRAWAL OF TROOPS FROM KUWAIT...

SCOTTY, I WANT TO TALK TO YOU ABOUT SOMETHING...

I JUST WANT YOU TO HEAR ME OUT AND TRY TO KEEP AN OPEN MIND, OKAY?

YOU KNOW THAT PHIL AND I HAVE BEEN SPENDING A LOT OF TIME TOGETHER LATELY...

AND I FEEL VERY LUCKY THAT I MET HIM. IT'S BEEN A BIG CHANGE FOR ME.

I JUST WANTED TO SEE HOW *YOU* FELT ABOUT HIM BECOMING MORE... A PART OF OUR LIVES.

NOW, I DON'T WANT YOU TO THINK I'M TRYING TO... *REPLACE* DAD IN ANY WAY...

WHAT DO YOU MEAN?

THAT'S *EXACTLY* WHAT YOU'RE TRYING TO DO.

≥SIGH≤

IS IT SO HARD FOR YOU TO BE JUST A LITTLE BIT SUPPORTIVE AND... OPTIMISTIC ABOUT ALL THIS?

: SKKRK : PARDON THE INTERRUPTION, BUT THIS IS PRINCIPAL JARMAN SPEAKING. IF I COULD PLEASE HAVE EVERYONE'S ATTENTION...

WE HAVE A, UH, UNEXPECTED SITUATION ON OUR HANDS. FACULTY, COULD YOU PLEASE HAVE ALL YOUR STUDENTS FILE OUT TO THE SOCCER FIELD IMMEDIATELY?

I HEARD SOMEONE CALLED IN A BOMB THREAT!

DUDE! THEY ACTUALLY FOUND THE BOMB ON CAMPUS!

ALL THE WAY OUT TO THE SOCCER FIELD, GUYS! KEEP MOVING!

PRETTY WEIRD, HUH?

OH, HEY.

IF THERE REALLY IS A BOMB, DON'T YOU THINK THEY'RE KIND OF ENDANGERING OUR LIVES BY KEEPING US HERE?

YEAH...BUT THINK HOW AMAZING IT WOULD BE IF WE ACTUALLY GOT TO SEE THE SCHOOL BLOW UP!

YOU SURE YOU WANT TO BE SEEN SITTING WITH ME?

TCH... SHUT UP.

SO IT LOOKS LIKE I'M GONNA BE MOVING PRETTY SOON.

WHAT?

I'M MOVING WITH MY MOM AND BROTHER... TO L.A. PROBABLY.

ARE YOU SERIOUS? WHY?

:SIGH: IT'S REALLY FUCKED-UP AND COMPLICATED, BUT BASICALLY... WE'RE, LIKE, LEAVING MY DAD.

HE DOESN'T EVEN KNOW YET.

BUT WHAT HAPPENED? I MEAN...

PFF...I DON'T REALLY WANT TO GET INTO IT, BUT...

I DON'T KNOW...I'M KIND OF HAPPY ABOUT IT. I'M SICK OF THIS SHIT-HOLE.

GREAT.

WELL, I GUESS IT'S BACK TO EATING LUNCH IN THE DARKROOM.

WHAT?

THAT'S WHAT I USED TO DO BEFORE I MET ALEX. I'D EAT MY LUNCH IN THE DARKROOM AND PRETEND TO PRINT PHOTOS.

YOU KNOW... THAT WAY I WOULDN'T HAVE TO SIT ON THE QUAD BY MYSELF.

OH MY GOD... THAT'S SO PATHETIC!

YEAH, WELL...

GOD, I CAN'T BELIEVE THIS!

OH, YOU'RE GOING TO BE FINE. YOU'LL MEET NEW PEOPLE...

CAMMIE... I DON'T **WANT** TO MEET NEW PEOPLE.

LISTEN UP! THE SHERIFF'S DEPARTMENT HAS ASSURED US THAT THE SITUATION IS UNDER CONTROL...BUT AS A PRECAUTION, WE ARE GOING TO DISMISS CLASS FOR THE REST OF THE DAY!

PLEASE LEAVE THE CAMPUS IN A QUICK AND ORDERLY MANNER, AND WE'LL SEE YOU BACK HERE TOMORROW!

DING!

I MADE THESE LITTLE PIZZA THINGS...

IT'S LIKE, AN ENGLISH MUFFIN WITH...

UH...

SO *THIS* IS A PRETTY INTEREST-ING MAGAZINE...

YEAH... I HAVE A SUBSCRIPTION.

THEY HAVE THIS ONE, UH, MUSIC COLUMNIST THAT'S PRETTY GOOD...

HUH...

WELL, HOW COME ALL YOUR OTHER MAGAZINES ARE STACKED NEATLY ON THAT SHELF, BUT THIS ONE WAS HIDDEN BETWEEN YOUR BED AND NIGHTSTAND?

IT WASN'T "HIDDEN." HERE...I'LL PUT IT BACK.

OH WAIT...

"SPLENDOR IN THE GRASS." HMM...A BUNCH OF PHOTOS OF DREW BARRYMORE AND HER GIRLFRIENDS...

LET ME HAVE IT.

OH MY GOD! THEY'RE NAKED!

THEY'RE ALL IN A POOL AND THEY'RE HUGGING AND—

GIVE IT!

HA HA HA HA HA

DON'T GET ALL PISSED OFF, SCOTTY. IT'S CUTE!

OH, NOW YOU HATE ME, RIGHT?

MAYBE WE SHOULD TURN ON THE NEWS...

YOU KNOW... SEE IF THE SCHOOL BLEW UP, OR...

DO YOU WANT TO SEE ME NAKED?

WHAT?

I SAID, "DO YOU WANT TO SEE ME NAKED?"

WHAT ARE YOU TALKING ABOUT?

I DON'T...

I'M JUST ASKING A QUESTION.

YES OR NO?

JESUS... MAYBE WE WERE RIGHT ABOUT YOU AFTER ALL!

LOOK, JUST FORGET—

YES.

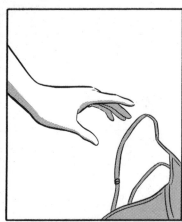